Design: Jill Coote
Recipe Photography: Peter Barry
Jacket and Illustration Artwork: Jane Winton,
courtesy of Bernard Thornton Artists, London
Editors: Jillian Stewart, Kate Cranshaw and Laura Potts

CLB 3514
This edition published in 1994 by
Whitecap Books Ltd., 1086 West 3rd Street,
North Vancouver, B.C., Canada V7P 3JS
© 1994 CLB Publishing,
Godalming, Surrey, England.
All rights reserved.
Printed and bound in Singapore
Published 1994
ISBN 1-55110-202-1

THE
LITTLE BOOK
·OF·

# Barbecues

*A selection of innovative barbecue recipes*
*to help you to make the most of summer*
*cookery.*

WHITECAP
BOOKS

# Introduction

With the glorious days and warm evenings of summer come long lunches and dinners eaten out doors. Eating *al fresco* is both relaxed and informal and it is a style of eating that continues to grow in popularity. Certainly it is hard to beat the taste of food cooked over an open broiler and the distinctive smell of barbecued food is one of the most evocative of summer.

There are two basic categories into which barbecues can be divided. At its most basic, a barbecue need only be an old gridiron resting on some bricks over a heat source. Home-made, open barbecues like these are inexpensive and effective, though it can be difficult to control temperature on them. More sophisticated open barbecues can be bought commercially and range in size from the small hibachi type to the larger trolley barbecues. Covered barbecues, such as kettle barbecues and gas broilers, make up the second category. They convect heat and cook in much the same way as a traditional oven rather than through direct heat as in an open, broiler barbecue. This is the classic Texas barbecue, which uses indirect heat. The Texas-style barbecue is easier to use at home because temperature and cooking time are easier to gauge.

There are several types of fuel that can be used for barbecuing, each of which has its advocates. For big broiler barbecues, wood can be used. Favorite woods are hickory and mesquite. It is important

to ensure that it is really dry before you begin. To get the very best results when using wood as your fuel, do not start cooking until the flames have died down and the wood has become embers. This ensures that the food does not get scorched. Charcoal and barbecue brickettes are the most commonly used form of barbecue fuel. They have the advantage over wood in that you can accurately judge just how long you are going to need to be able to cook your food. By combining charcoal with barbecue brickettes it is possible to avoid the problem of fuel not lasting long enough to cook large pieces of meat – a problem that is common when using charcoal alone.

Though a good barbecue and reliable fuel are important to the success of a barbecued meal, careful preparation of the food is also vital. Food is cooked at a very high temperature on a barbecue and must be properly marinated first to ensure that it does not become tough or dried out in the cooking process. Marinades vary, though many are oil- and wine-based, with garlic, herbs, and spices added to give flavor.

This book provides a selection of delicious recipes that give new ideas on how to prepare meat, fish, and vegetables to barbecue, giving you the chance to experiment with new and delicious combinations of flavors rather than relying on tried and tested favorites.

# Monkfish and Pepper Kebobs with Bearnaise Butter Sauce

## SERVES 4

*Monkfish is a firm, succulent white fish, ideal for kebobs.*

PREPARATION: 30 mins
COOKING: 15-20 mins

8 slices Canadian bacon, rind removed
2 pieces lemongrass
2 pounds monkfish, cut into 2-inch pieces
1 green bell and 1 red bell pepper, cut into
    2-inch pieces
12 button mushrooms, washed and trimmed
8 bayleaves
Oil for brushing
½ cup dry white wine
4 tbsps tarragon vinegar
2 shallots, finely chopped
1 tbsp chopped fresh chervil or parsley
1 cup melted butter
Salt and pepper

**1.** Cut the bacon in half lengthwise and then in half across. Peel the lemongrass and use only the soft core. Cut this into small shreds.

**2.** Place a piece of fish on each piece of bacon and top with a shred of lemongrass. Roll up the bacon around the fish. Thread each roll onto

**Step 2** Place a piece of fish onto a strip of bacon and top with a shred of lemongrass. Roll and thread onto kebob skewers.

kebob skewers, alternating with the peppers, mushrooms, and bayleaves. Brush well with oil.

**3.** Cook on an oiled rack over hot coals 15-20 minutes, turning frequently and brushing with more oil, if necessary, until the fish is cooked.

**4.** Heat together the wine, vinegar, and shallots in a small saucepan until they are boiling. Cook rapidly until reduced by half.

**5.** Stir in the herbs and lower the heat. Beat in the butter, a little at a time, until the sauce is thick and creamy. Season to taste and serve with the kebobs.

# Turkey and Ham Rolls

*SERVES 4-6*

*Serve these stylish rolled turkey escalopes with a mixed green salad and rice.*

PREPARATION: 30 mins
COOKING: 20-30 mins

---

2 turkey breasts, 1 pound each, skinned
⅓ cup butter softened
1 clove garlic, crushed
1 tbsp oregano leaves
Salt and pepper
16 thin slices country or Smithfield ham
Oil

---

**1.** Cut the turkey breasts in half lengthwise. Place each piece between two sheets of dampened parchment paper and beat with a rolling-pin or steak hammer to flatten.

**2.** Mix the butter, garlic, oregano, and salt and pepper together.

**3.** Spread half of the mixture over each slice of turkey. Lay 4 slices of ham on top of each piece of turkey.

**4.** Roll each turkey escalope up, tucking in the sides, and tie with thread in 3 places. Spread the remaining garlic butter on the outside of each roll.

**5.** Cook the rolls over medium-hot coals for 20-30 minutes, or until tender. A meat thermometer inserted into the center of each roll should read 190°F.

**6.** Slice each roll into ½-inch rounds to serve.

# Scallop, Bacon, and Shrimp Kebobs

*SERVES 4*

*Don't overcook these kebobs or the scallops will become tough.*

PREPARATION: 25 mins
COOKING: 15-20 mins

---

12 large scallops
12 slices smoked Canadian bacon
12 raw jumbo shrimp, peeled and deveined
Juice of 1 lemon
2 tbsps oil
Coarsely ground black pepper

*Red chili yogurt sauce*
3 slices bread, crusts removed, soaked in water
2 cloves garlic, finely chopped
1 red chili, seeded and chopped
1 large canned red pimiento
3 tbsps olive oil
⅔ cup plain yogurt

---

**1.** Wrap each scallop in a slice of bacon and thread onto skewers, alternating with the shrimp.

**2.** Mix the lemon juice, oil, and pepper, and brush over the kebobs. Cook on a wire rack over medium hot coals 15-20 minutes. Turn frequently and cook until the bacon is lightly crisped and the scallops are just firm.

**3.** Meanwhile, prepare the sauce. Squeeze the bread to remove the water and place the bread in a blender.

**4.** Add the garlic, chili, and pimiento and blend well.

**5.** With the machine running, pour in the oil through the funnel in a thin, steady stream.

**6.** Keep the machine running until the mixture is a smooth, shiny paste.

**7.** Combine with the yogurt and mix well. Serve with the kebobs.

# Barbecued Steak

*SERVES 6*

*Cooking one large steak means that everyone gets fed at once!*

PREPARATION: 25 mins
COOKING: 30-45 mins

---

3½ pounds chuck steak

*Barbecue seasoning*
1½ tbsps salt
½ tsp freshly ground pepper
½ tsp Cayenne pepper (or paprika for a milder tasting mixture)

*Barbecue sauce*
4 tbsps oil
1½ cups tomato sauce
3 tbsps Worcestershire sauce
6 tbsps cider or wine vinegar
4 tbsps soft brown sugar
4 tbsps chopped onion
1 clove garlic, crushed
1 bayleaf
4 tbsps water
2 tsps mustard powder
Dash of Tabasco
Salt and pepper

---

**1.** First prepare the barbecue sauce. Combine all the ingredients, reserving salt and pepper to add later.

**2.** Cook the sauce in a heavy pan over a low heat for 30 minutes, stirring frequently and adding more water if the sauce reduces too quickly.

**3.** Remove the bayleaf and add salt and pepper to taste before using. The sauce should be thick.

**4.** Score the meat across both sides with a large knife. Mix together the barbecue seasoning and rub all over the meat.

**5.** Sear the meat on both sides on an oiled broiler rack just above the hot coals. Raise the rack, baste the meat with the barbecue sauce, and broil slowly 30-45 minutes, depending on taste.

**6.** During the last 5 minutes, lower the broiler rack and broil the meat quickly on both sides, still basting with the sauce.

**7.** Slice the meat thinly across the grain and serve with any remaining sauce.

# Lamb Kebobs

SERVES 4

*Meat kebobs are a typical Greek dish and these have all the characteristic flavors – oregano, garlic, lemon, and olive oil.*

PREPARATION: 20 mins, plus marinating
COOKING: 10-20 mins

---

1½ pounds lean lamb from the leg or neck fillet
Juice of 1 large lemon
6 tbsps olive oil
1 clove garlic, crushed
1 tbsp chopped fresh oregano
1 tbsp chopped fresh thyme
Salt and pepper
2 medium onions
Fresh bayleaves

---

**1.** Trim the meat of excess fat and cut it into 2-inch cubes. Mix together the remaining

**Step 1** Cut the meat into even-sized cubes.

**Step 3** Thread the meat and bayleaves onto skewers and slip the onion rings over the meat.

ingredients, except the bayleaves and the onions. Pour the mixture into a shallow dish.

**2.** Add the meat to the marinade and turn to coat completely. Cover and leave to marinate for at least four hours, or overnight.

**3.** To assemble the kebobs, remove the meat from the marinade and thread onto skewers, alternating with the fresh bayleaves.

**4.** Slice the onions into rings and slip the rings over the meat on the skewers.

**5.** Place the kebobs on the oiled broiler rack over hot coals, and broil about 5-10 minutes per side basting frequently. Pour over any remaining marinade to serve.

# Marsala Fish

*SERVES 4*

*Barbecued whole fish make a delicious alternative to burgers and kebobs.*

PREPARATION: 25 mins
COOKING: 10-15 mins

---

4 medium mackerel, trout, or similar whole
　fish, cleaned
2 tsps turmeric
⅛ tsp ground cinnamon
⅛ tsp ground cloves
1 small piece ginger, grated
Juice of 1 lemon
2 green chilies, finely chopped
1 clove garlic, crushed
Salt and pepper
Fresh coriander leaves

*Accompaniment*
1 cucumber, finely diced

⅔ cup thick-set plain yogurt
1 green onion (scallion), finely chopped
Salt and pepper

---

**1.** Cut three slits into each side of the fish. Combine the spices, lemon juice, oil, garlic, chilies, and salt and pepper, and spread over the fish and inside the cuts.

**2.** Place whole sprigs of coriander inside the fish. Brush the broiler rack lightly with oil or use a wire fish rack.

**3.** Cook the fish 10-15 minutes, turning often and basting with any remaining mixture.

**4.** Combine the accompaniment ingredients and serve with the fish.

# Zanzibar Shrimp

*SERVES 4*

*Jumbo shrimp make impressive kebobs.*

PREPARATION: 25 mins
COOKING: 18-23 mins

1 pound jumbo shrimp, peeled and deveined
1 large fresh pineapple, peeled, cored, and cut
   into chunks
Oil

*Sauce*
Remaining pineapple
⅔ cup orange juice
1 tbsp vinegar
1 tbsp lime juice
1 tsp mustard powder
1 tbsp brown sugar

*To serve*
4 tbsps flaked coconut
Endive or lettuce leaves

**1.** Alternately thread the shrimp and pineapple pieces onto skewers, using about 4 pineapple pieces per skewer.

**2.** Place the remaining pineapple and the rest of the sauce ingredients into a food processor and purée.

**3.** Pour into a small pan and cook over low heat about 10-15 minutes to reduce slightly.

**4.** Place the kebobs on a lightly-oiled rack above medium hot coals and cook about 6 minutes, turning and basting frequently with the sauce.

**5.** Sprinkle the cooked kebobs with a little shredded coconut and serve on endive or lettuce leaves. Serve the remaining sauce separately.

# Seekh Kebobs

*MAKES 18*

*These spicy Indian kebobs are delicious.*

PREPARATION: 15-20 mins
COOKING: 12-16 mins

Juice of ½ lemon
2 tbsps minced fresh mint
3-4 tbsps minced coriander leaves
1 tbsp raw cashew nuts
1 medium onion, coarsely chopped
2 cloves garlic, chopped
1-2 fresh green chilies, seeded and finely
    chopped
1½ pounds lean ground beef or lamb
2 tsps ground coriander seeds
2 tsps ground cumin seeds
1 tsp ground caraway seeds
½ tsp garam masala
½ tsp annatto
1 egg yolk
¼ tsp chili powder
Salt and pepper

*Grind the following ingredients in a coffee or
    spice grinder:*

2 tbsps white poppyseeds
2 tbsps sesame seeds

**1.** Put the first seven ingredients into a liquidizer and blend to a smooth paste. Transfer the mixture to a large bowl.

**2.** Using the liquidizer, grind the meat in 2-3 batches until it is a smooth paste; add to the liquidized ingredients in the bowl.

**3.** Add the rest of the ingredients and process in a food processor until the mixture is smooth.

**4.** Chill 30 minutes.

**5.** Divide the mix into 18 balls.

**6.** Mold each ball onto a skewer and form into a sausage shape about 4-5 inches long.

**7.** Brush generously with oil and place on an oiled rack just above coals. Cook 6-8 minutes, brush with more oil, and cook for a further 6-8 minutes.

# Mustard Broiled Pork with Poppyseeds

*SERVES 4-6*

*To serve the pork, slice thinly and accompany with the remaining sauce.*

PREPARATION: 20 mins, plus marinating
COOKING: 45 mins-1 hr

6-7 ounces whole pork tenderloin
2 tbsps poppyseeds

*Marinade*
1 tbsp mild mustard
4 tbsps olive oil
4 tbsps unsweetened apple juice
1 clove garlic, crushed
Salt and pepper

*Sweet mustard sauce*
1¼ cups American or French mustard
½ cup light brown sugar
4 tbsps cider
2 tsps chopped fresh tarragon
Pinch chili pepper
Salt

**1.** Mix the marinade ingredients together and rub into the pork. Place in a dish, cover, and refrigerate for 4 hours or overnight.

**2.** Using a barbecue with an adjustable broiler rack, place the pork over the coals on the highest level. Cook for 45 minutes-1 hour, basting with the marinade and turning frequently.

**3.** Lower the shelf and baste frequently with the sauce during the last 10 minutes of cooking time.

**4.** During the last 5 minutes, sprinkle the pork fillets with the poppyseeds.

**5.** Combine the sauce ingredients, adding salt to taste. Serve with the broiled pork.

# Boti Kebobs

*SERVES 6*

*Tender, boneless lamb is the traditional meat used for these Indian kebobs.*

PREPARATION: 20 mins, plus marinating
COOKING: 16-22 mins

---

1½ pounds boned leg of lamb
2 cloves garlic, chopped
2 tbsps chopped coriander leaves
2 tbsps lemon juice
3 tbsps thick-set plain yogurt
Salt to taste
½ tsp ground turmeric

*Grind the following 4 ingredients in a coffee grinder:*

6 green cardamom pods
1-inch cinnamon stick
2-3 dried red chilies
1 tbsp coriander seeds

---

**1.** Prick the meat all over with a sharp knife and cut into 1½-inch cubes.

**2.** Put the garlic, coriander leaves, lemon juice, and yogurt into a liquidizer or food processor and blend until smooth. Add all the remaining ingredients.

**3.** Put the meat into a bowl and add the liquidized ingredients. Mix thoroughly, cover and leave to marinate 6-8 hours.

**4.** Thread the meat onto skewers leaving about a ¼-inch gap between each piece. Mix any remaining marinade with 2 tbsps oil and reserve.

**5.** Place the skewers on an oiled broiler rack over medium hot coals and broil 2-3 minutes on each side. Adjust the rack to the top position. Brush the kebobs with the marinade mixture and broil 6-8 minutes. Repeat for the other side.

# Indian Chicken

*SERVES 4-6*

*Spiced yogurt makes a delicious coating for chicken pieces.*

PREPARATION: 15 mins, plus marinating
COOKING: 45-55 mins

---

1 × 3-pound chicken, cut into 8 pieces
2¼ cups plain yogurt
2 tsps ground coriander
2 tsps paprika
1 tsp ground turmeric
Juice of 1 lime
1 tbsp honey
½ clove garlic, crushed
1 small piece fresh ginger, peeled and grated

---

**1.** Pierce the chicken all over with a fork or skewer. Combine all the remaining ingredients, and spread half the mixture over the chicken, rubbing in well.

**2.** Place the chicken in a shallow dish or a plastic bag and cover or tie and leave for at least 4 hours or overnight in the refrigerator.

**3.** Using a barbecue with an adjustable rack, arrange the chicken, skin side down, and broil on the level furthest from the coals. Broil 15-20 minutes or until lightly browned, turn over and cook again until lightly browned. Baste frequently with the remaining marinade.

**4.** Lower the broiler for the last 15 minutes and cook, turning and basting frequently, until the chicken is brown and the skin is crisp.

**5.** Serve any remaining yogurt mixture separately as a sauce.

# Sausage, Apple, & Pepper Kebobs

### SERVES 6

*Perfect for summer barbecues, these kebobs are unusual, easy, and inexpensive.*

PREPARATION: 15 mins plus marinating
COOKING: 5-6 mins

---

⅔ cup thick honey
1 tsp chopped fresh dill
½ cup white wine vinegar
1 pound mortadella, cut in 2-inch pieces
2 large tart apples
1 large red bell pepper

---

**Step 3** Cut peppers in half and remove the core and seeds. Also cut out any white parts as these tend to be bitter.

**1.** Mix together the honey and dill. Gradually whisk in the vinegar to blend thoroughly. Add the sausage, stirring to coat evenly, and allow to marinate about 2 hours.

**Step 1** Mix the honey and herbs together and gradually beat in the vinegar.

**2.** Cut the apples in quarters and remove the cores. Cut in half again crosswise or lengthwise.

**3.** Cut the pepper in half. Chop into pieces about the same size as the sausage and apple.

**4.** Thread the ingredients onto skewers, alternating the pepper, sausage and apple.

**5.** Brush with the marinade and place over hot coals on an oiled broiler rack. Cook about 5-6 minutes, turning 2 or 3 times, and brushing frequently with the marinade. Pour any additional marinade over the kebobs before serving.

# Pork Burgers

SERVES 4

*This recipe uses lean ground pork, and so makes for a healthier burger.*

PREPARATION: 20 mins
COOKING: 15 mins

---

1 pound extra lean, raw ground pork
1 small onion, finely chopped
½ cup fresh wholewheat breadcrumbs
1 meat cube, crumbled
1 tsp chopped fresh parsley
Salt and black pepper, to taste
1 tbsp tomato paste
1 tsp American or French mustard
1 egg, beaten

*To serve*
4 wholewheat burger rolls
Crisp lettuce leaves and tomato and cucumber
    slices

---

**1.** In a large bowl, mix together the ground
pork, onion, and breadcrumbs.

**Step 2** Add the remaining burger ingredients to the ground meat and onion mixture. Mix them together thoroughly.

**2.** Stir in all the remaining burger ingredients
and mix together thoroughly. Divide into
quarters, and form each into a hamburger patty
with lightly-floured hands.

**3.** Arrange the burgers on an oiled broiler rack
and cook over hot coals 7-8 minutes on each
side, turning the burgers to prevent them
burning.

**4.** Serve in wholewheat rolls with lettuce,
sliced tomato, and cucumber.

# Turkey Kebobs

## SERVES 6

*These economical kebobs are healthy, low-fat, and perfect for an informal gathering.*

PREPARATION: 20 mins, plus marinating
COOKING: 20-30 mins

3 pounds white turkey meat
2 tsps fresh chopped sage
1 sprig rosemary, chopped
Juice 1 lemon
2 tbsps olive oil
Salt and freshly ground black pepper
4 slices Canadian bacon, rind removed
Whole sage leaves

**1.** Remove any bone from the turkey and cut the meat into even-sized cubes.

**2.** Put the chopped sage, rosemary, lemon

**Step 3** Cut the bacon in half lengthwise and again crosswise.

**Step 4**
Carefully roll the marinated turkey in the strips of bacon.

juice, oil, salt, and pepper into a large bowl and stir in the turkey meat, mixing well to coat evenly. Cover and refrigerate overnight.

**3.** Cut the bacon slices in half lengthwise and then crosswise.

**4.** Wrap these pieces around as many of the cubes of marinated turkey meat as possible.

**5.** Thread the turkey-and-bacon rolls alternately with the whole sage leaves and any unwrapped turkey cubes onto kebob skewers.

**6.** Cook the kebobs over medium-hot coals 20-30 minutes, turning frequently and basting with the marinade whilst cooking. Serve immediately.

# Niçoise Chicken

SERVES 4

*In this recipe, a raw tomato sauce makes the perfect accompaniment to olive-stuffed chicken.*

PREPARATION: 30 mins, plus chilling
COOKING: 20-25 mins

4 boned chicken breasts, unskinned
4 tbsps oil
2 tbsps lemon juice

*Filling*
1 pound large black olives, pitted
2 tbsps capers
1 clove garlic, roughly chopped
4 canned anchovy fillets
2 tbsps olive oil

*Sauce*
1 pound ripe tomatoes, skinned, seeded and chopped
1 shallot, minced
2 tbsps minced parsley
2 tbsps minced basil
2 tbsps white wine vinegar
2 tbsps olive oil
1 tbsp sugar

Salt and pepper
1 tbsp tomato paste

**1.** Cut a pocket into the thickest side of each of the chicken breasts.

**2.** Combine half the olives, half the capers, and the remaining ingredients for the filling in a blender or food processor.

**3.** Work to a paste. Add the remaining olives and capers and process a few times to chop them roughly.

**4.** Fill the chicken breasts with the mixture and chill to help firm.

**5.** Baste the skin side of the chicken with the oil and lemon juice mixed together. Cook skin side down first for 10-15 minutes over medium hot coals.

**6.** Turn over, baste again and broil another 10 minutes on the other side.

**7.** Meanwhile, combine the sauce ingredients and mix together very well. Serve with the chicken.

# Swordfish Kebobs

*SERVES 4-6*

*Swordfish is a firm-fleshed fish, so it won't fall apart during cooking.*

PREPARATION: 15 mins
COOKING: 10 mins

---

2¼ pounds swordfish steaks
6 tbsps olive oil
1 tsp chopped oregano
1 tsp chopped marjoram
Juice and rind of ½ lemon
4 tomatoes, cut in thick slices
2 lemons, cut in thin slices
Salt and freshly ground pepper
Lemon slices and parsley, for garnish

---

**Step 1** Cut the swordfish steaks into even-sized pieces.

**Step 3** Thread the ingredients onto the skewers, alternating the colors.

**1.** Cut the swordfish steaks into 2-inch pieces.

**2.** Mix the olive oil, herbs, lemon juice, and rind together and set it aside.

**3.** Thread the swordfish, tomato slices, and lemon slices onto skewers, alternating the ingredients.

**4.** Brush the skewers with the oil and lemon juice mixture, and cook on an oiled broiler rack over hot coals about 10 minutes, basting frequently with the lemon and oil.

**5.** Serve garnished with lemon slices and parsley.

# *Butterflied Lamb*

*SERVES 6-8*

*To make preparation easy, get a butcher to "butterfly" the lamb for you.*

PREPARATION: 40 mins, plus marinating
overnight
COOKING: 40-50 mins

---

4 pounds leg of lamb on the bone
5 tbsps oil
Juice and rind of one lemon
Small bunch mint, roughly chopped
Salt and coarsely ground black pepper
1 clove garlic, crushed

---

**1.** To butterfly the lamb, cut through the skin along the line of the main bone, right down to the bone.

**2.** Cut the meat away from the bone, opening out the leg while scraping against the bone with a small, sharp knife. Take out the bone and remove the excess fat.

**3.** Flatten thick parts by beating with a rolling-pin or steak hammer.

**4.** Alternatively, make shallow cuts halfway through the thickest parts and press open.

**5.** Thread two or three long skewers through the meat – this will make the meat easier to handle and turn on the broiler.

**6.** Place in a large, shallow dish. Mix the other ingredients together and pour the mixture over the lamb, rubbing it in well.

**7.** Cover the dish and refrigerate overnight. Turn the lamb frequently.

**8.** Remove the lamb from the dish and reserve the marinade.

**9.** Broil at least 6 inches away from the flame, on the skin side first. Broil for 20 minutes per side for rare lamb and 30-40 minutes per side for more well cooked meat.

**10.** Baste frequently during broiling. Remove the skewers and cut the slices across the grain to serve.

**11.** Alternatively, roast the lamb in a 350°F oven for half of the cooking time and broil on the barbecue for the last half of cooking.

# Mexican Kebobs

*SERVES 4*

*The spice mixture and sauce give these their Mexican flavor. Serve with rice or tortillas and taco sauce.*

PREPARATION: 15 mins, plus marinating
COOKING: 15-20 mins

---

1 pound pork or beef, cut into 2-inch pieces
1 cup large button mushrooms, left whole
2 medium onions, quartered
8 bayleaves
1 tsp cocoa powder
2 tsps chili powder
¼ tsp garlic powder
½ tsp dried marjoram
Salt and pepper
6 tbsps oil

---

**1.** Put meat and mushrooms in a bowl, add the remaining ingredients, and stir to coat well.

**2.** Cover the bowl and leave to marinate at least 6 hours, preferably overnight.

**3.** Remove the meat, mushrooms, and bayleaves from the marinade and reserve it. Thread onto skewers, alternating meat, onions, mushrooms, and bayleaves.

**Step 1** Place meat and mushrooms in a deep bowl with the marinade ingredients and stir to coat thoroughly.

**4.** Place on an oiled broiler rack over hot coals 15-20 minutes, turning and basting frequently. The lamb may be served pink.

**Step 3** Thread the meat and mushrooms onto skewers, alternating with onions and bayleaves.

# Index

Scallop, Bacon, and Shrimp Kebobs